Winston Churchill

Iain Finlayson

Illustrated by
Peter Gregory

Hamish Hamilton
London

First published 1980 by
Hamish Hamilton Children's Books
Garden House, 57-59 Long Acre, London WC2E 9JZ
© text 1980 by Iain Finlayson
© illustrations 1980 Hamish Hamilton Ltd

British Library Cataloguing in Publication Data

Finlayson, Iain
Winston Churchill. — (Profiles).
1.   Churchill, *Sir* Winston, b.1847 —
Juvenile literature
2.   Prime ministers — Great Britain —
Biography — Juvenile literature
I.   Series
941.082′092′4   DA566.9.C5

ISBN 0-241-10482-3

Typeset by Pioneer
Printed in Great Britain by
Ebenezer Baylis & Son Ltd.,
The Trinity Press, Worcester and London

Chapter One

On Monday 30 November 1874, at 1.30 a.m., Winston Leonard Spencer Churchill was born in Blenheim Palace. It was not at all what his parents, Lord and Lady Randolph Churchill, had intended. They had expected their first child to be born at the end of January, two months later, in their London house at 48 Charles Street. But from the very beginning, young Winston was showing that he had a will of his own. What better place to be born than in the great house given by the nation to his glorious ancestor John Churchill, 1st Duke of Marlborough, one of England's greatest soldiers?

Winston immediately began to make a fuss. As a baby he was dark-eyed, dark-haired, and had a powerful pair of lungs. Hearing her grandson shout, the Duchess of Marlborough declared, 'I have myself given birth to quite a number of infants. They were all pretty vocal when they arrived, but such an earth-shaking noise as this newborn baby made I have never heard!' Winston's father was a rising young politician, who had been elected to Parliament in 1874. He was the second surviving son of Winston's grandfather, the 7th Duke of Marlborough. Randolph, who had met and married

the beautiful Jennie Jerome, daughter of a wild, self-made American millionaire who regularly won and lost several fortunes, seemed set for a long and brilliant political career. With Jennie, he moved easily through a glittering and aristocratic social world in which the Prince of Wales was a familiar, cheerful figure.

Winston was born into a world that has vanished, the era of Queen Victoria 'when the structure of our country seemed firmly set, when its position in trade and on the seas was unrivalled, and when the realization of the greatness of our Empire and of our duty to preserve it was ever growing stronger.' Looking back to the time of his birth, Winston Churchill saw the British people then as lords and colonists of vast areas of the globe. 'They thought they could teach the world the art of government, and the science of economics. They

were sure they were supreme at sea and consequently safe at home.'

In 1874, the British Empire was at the height of its glory. It ruled lands and peoples throughout the world, it was safe from attack at home and undefeated on the high seas. Britain was rich, proud, powerful, secure, sometimes arrogant, and it seemed as though the British were destined to rule over their countless colonies and possessions for evermore. But like a fiery rocket, dazzling and brilliant, the British Empire had soared to a magnificent peak from which it could only decline. The world of Winston's father and grandfather was already dying. Randolph's son, born at the end of one era, would have to live most of his long life in the very different age of the 20th century. As a warrior, politician, and statesman, Winston would preside over the slow decline of the class and the country into which he had been born.

In 1876, Winston, with his father and mother, went to Dublin with the Duke of Marlborough who was to be Lord Lieutenant of Ireland. Aged three, Winston's first memory was of his grandfather unveiling a statue. 'A great black crowd, scarlet soldiers on horseback, strings pulling away a brown, shiny sheet, the old Duke, the formidable grandpapa, talking loudly to the crowd.' He remembered his mother, too, dashing about the country on horseback. 'My picture of her in Ireland is in a riding habit, fitting like a skin, and often beautifully spotted with mud.' Winston's young mother was widely reckoned to be one of the most beautiful women of her day, and to her son she seemed like 'a fairy princess: a radiant being possessed of limitless riches and power. She shone for me like the Evening Star. I loved her dearly — but at a distance.'

At a distance. How remote Jennie and Lord Randolph must have seemed to their son. Winston's childhood was not happy. His parents were not unkind, but they were thoughtless and neglectful. They were young, successful, and popular. They led a hectic social life that did not include children. Living a life of wealth and privilege, they had no time or patience for the boring details of domestic cares. Winston was saved from loneliness by his nurse, whom he nicknamed 'Woomany'. 'Mrs Everest it was who looked after me and tended all my wants. It was to her I poured out my many troubles.' Lord Randolph was impatient with his son, and called him 'that boy!' He seemed hardly to notice Winston at all for long periods, and when he did it was only to find fault. Winston himself admitted, 'I was what people call a troublesome boy.'

If he was troublesome at home, he was even more of a problem at school. In 1882, Winston was sent to a school in Ascot. There he was more miserable than at any other time in his life. 'How I hated this school, and what a life of anxiety I lived there for more than two years. I made very little progress at my lessons, and none at all at games. I counted the days and the hours to the end of every term.' He wasn't stupid — just totally unable to take an interest in the lessons. He enjoyed reading and finding out things for himself, but rebelled at authority and discipline. The school's discipline was brutal. 'Two or three times a month the whole school was marshalled in the Library, and one or more delinquents were hauled off to an adjoining apartment by the two head boys, and there flogged until they bled freely, while the rest sat quaking, listening to their screams.'

Winston was accused of 'phenomenal slovenliness' and 'negligence'. He was once flogged for stealing sugar, but took revenge by kicking the headmaster's prized straw hat to bits. For a while, he was the hero of the school. But finally he fell ill, and his parents realized that he must be taken away from the school. At his next school, he nearly died of pneumonia, but recovered and began to enjoy subjects such as French and History, memorising poetry, and not only learned to swim but now began to develop his lasting love of horses and riding. At the age of 12, he was sent to

school at Harrow where for more than four years he came bottom of every class. His only successes were winning prizes for fencing and being able to recite 1200 lines of Macaulay's poem 'Lays of Ancient Rome' from memory. He also developed a deep love for the English language at Harrow and later in his life he stoutly

defended the ordinary English sentence as 'a noble thing.'

Winston was not good looking. He had curly red hair, blue eyes, a short and sturdy body, freckles, a snub nose, and he spoke with a slight lisp and stammer. But he was afraid of nothing and nobody. He was sure of himself, brave, obstinate, and boisterous. Nothing could keep him down for long. He stood his ground even when he volunteered to let a great swordsman, who had come to visit the school, balance an apple on his head and cut it in half with one swipe of cold steel. At home, he had a huge collection of lead soldiers and used to play war games with his private army, setting them up in regiments and planning campaigns. These toy soldiers, 1500 of them, were to help decide young Winston's whole future. Lord Randolph Churchill had resigned as Chancellor of the Exchequer and Leader of the House of Commons after a minor quarrel. His political career seemed to be in ruins, and he was already beginning to suffer the first symptoms of the disease that was to kill him, horribly, in 1895. He began to worry about his son.

What was Winston fit for? Not much, to judge by his school reports. Here he was, 15 years old, a dunce at school, no obvious talents, and not likely to make a go of university. Neither his father nor his mother had paid much attention to Winston until now. But something had to be done about him soon. In Winston's own words, 'the day came when my father paid a formal visit of inspection. All the troops [of lead soldiers] were arranged in the correct formation of attack. He spent twenty minutes studying the scene — which was really impressive — with a keen eye and a captivating smile. At the end he asked me if I would like to go into the Army. I thought it would be splendid to command an Army, so I said 'Yes' at once: and immediately I was taken at my word.'

From that time on, Winston followed the 'Army Class' course at Harrow which was intended to prepare him for entrance to the Royal Military Academy at Sandhurst. Twice he failed the entrance examination, and almost gave up hope. He was sent to a London school which specialised in tutoring young men for the exam, but before beginning to study he took a winter holiday at Bournemouth where, during a game of 'Follow My Leader', he managed to jump off a bridge, 9 metres to the ground, and knocked himself unconscious for three days. It was a blessing in disguise, because during months of convalescence he was able to do a lot of work on mathematics and, at the third attempt, managed to scrape through the entrance exam for Sandhurst.

He qualified for a cavalry cadetship, and was overjoyed at the thought of having his own horse and a magnificent uniform. But Lord Randolph was frankly disappointed. He had hoped that Winston would do well enough in the exam to qualify to join an infantry battalion, and had already been in touch with the Duke of Cambridge, Colonel-in-Chief of the 60th Rifles, to arrange the matter. Winston, who was delighted to have passed the exam at all, received a letter from his father, 'a long and very severe letter, expressing the bleakest view of my educational career, showing a marked lack of appreciation at my success in the examination, which he suggested I had only scraped through, and warning me of the danger in which I plainly lay of becoming a "social wastrel".' Lord Randolph told his son that he was destined to lead 'a shabby, unhappy and futile existence', due to Winston's 'slovenly, happy-go-lucky, harum scarum style of work.'

Winston was hurt and upset by this cheerless letter, but promised that he would do well at Sandhurst. His father's coldness and lack of enthusiasm could not dampen the great joy that bubbled up in Winston at the thought of becoming 'a real live cavalry officer in no more than 18 months.' He was not depressed by his failure as a schoolboy; all his good nature, cheerfulness, and natural optimism came to his rescue. It was adventure he looked forward to, and a life of action. At Sandhurst, he thought, he would have a new start.

Chapter Two

At Sandhurst everyone started equal. It didn't matter that Winston knew very little about French, Latin or Mathematics. But he did, at last, have to buckle down and accept strict discipline. Luckily, he enjoyed and worked hard at classes in mapmaking, tactics, fortifications, and military law. He was interested and excited by his new life. Every day there were long hours of study and parade, drill, gymnastics and riding. 'We dug trenches, constructed breastworks, revetted parapets with sandbags . . . cut railway lines with slabs of guncotton, and learned how to blow up masonry, bridges, or make substitutes out of pontoons or timber. We drew maps of all the hills round Camberley, made road reconnaissances in every direction, and set out picket lines and paper plans for advanced guards or rear guards, and even did some very simple tactical schemes.'

The world in 1893 was an exciting place for a young officer in the British Army. Winston looked around and discovered that 'there were still savage and barbarous peoples. There were Zulus and Afghans, also the Dervishes of the Sudan. Some of these might, if they were well-disposed, 'put up a show' some day.

There might even be a mutiny or a revolt in India. . . . we should all get our commissions so much earlier and march about the plains of India and win medals and distinction, and perhaps rise to very high command like Clive when quite young!' Mostly, Winston enjoyed riding, his greatest pleasure at Sandhurst. 'I and the group in which I moved spent all our money on hiring horses . . . We organized point-to-points and even a steeplechase and bucketted gaily about the countryside. . . . No hour of life is lost that is spent in the saddle.'

Winston's good showing at Sandhurst even impressed his father and they became more friendly with one another. Lord Randolph began introducing his son to important politicians and other influential friends. But just as their relationship seemed to be improving, Winston's father died on 24 January 1895. Winston was 20 years old, and for the rest of his life felt that death had robbed him of the chance to prove his worth to his father and to be friends with him on equal terms, man to man. In February, a month later, he passed out from Sandhurst with honours, eighth in his class of 150. It had been a hard but happy experience for Winston, and he immediately obtained a commission in a cavalry regiment, the 4th Hussars.

On a salary of £120 a year, he was at last his own master and a success. The world opened for him 'like Aladdin's cave' and he began a life of action and adventure. Looking back, Winston later wrote, 'From the beginning of 1895 . . . I have never had time to turn round. I could almost count on my fingers the days when I have had nothing to do. . . . All the days were

16

good and each day better than the other.' He gave this advice to all young men like himself, 'Don't take No for an answer. Never submit to failure. Do not be fobbed off with mere personal success or acceptance. You will make all kinds of mistakes: but as long as you are generous and true, and also fierce, you cannot hurt the world or even seriously distress her. She was made to be wooed and won by youth.'

He didn't have to wait long for excitement. The world was, by and large, quite peaceful but there was a minor battle in Cuba between Spanish soldiers and native guerilla fighters. Winston pushed himself forward at once. He obtained leave from his regiment and a job as a war correspondent for a newspaper. At

17

the beginning of November 1895 he sailed off for Havana, the capital of Cuba. He set eyes on the island early one morning and 'felt as if I sailed with Long John Silver and first gazed on Treasure Island. Here was a place where real things were going on.' It was his first sight of battle and on his 21st birthday he heard shots fired in anger for the first (but not the last) time in his life. He didn't take active part in the fighting, but he loved the sense of adventure that rose in his heart by being with other men 'on our horses, in uniform; our revolvers loaded. In the dusk and half-light, long files of armed and laden men are shuffling off towards the enemy. He may be very near; perhaps he is waiting for us a mile away.' Winston, although not very impressed by the conduct of this inefficiently run little skirmish, was enthralled and eager for more.

His next brush with bullets and cold steel was in India where Pathan tribesmen had risen against the British army at Malakand in Afghanistan. Winston again got himself a job as a war correspondent — this time for the *Daily Telegraph* — and joined the forces led by Sir Bindon Blood who proceeded to crush the rebellion. Winston was hoping for adventure and for something exciting to happen — it did! 'Suddenly the mountainside sprang to life. Swords flashed from behind rocks, bright flags waved here and there. Loud explosions resounded close at hand. From high up on the crag, one thousand, two thousand, three thousand feet above us, white or blue figures appeared, dropping down the mountainside from ledge to ledge like monkeys down the branches of a tall tree. A shrill crying arose from many points. Yi! Yi! Yi! Bang! Bang! Bang! The hostile figures continued to flow down the mountain side, and scores began to gather in rocks about a hundred yards away from us. I began to shoot carefully at the men gathering in the rocks. A lot of bullets whistled about us. But we lay very flat, and no harm was done. We had certainly found the adventure for which we had been looking.' Winston began to believe that he was at last a winner. 'I have faith in my star,' he wrote. 'I am intended to do something in the world.' He wanted to win a medal, and he was mentioned in dispatches for bravely but rashly trying to rescue a wounded man during this campaign. To do it, he had to kill four of the enemy in his way. He longed to make a reputation for personal courage more than anything else in the world.

In 1898 he published his first book, an account of the Malakand campaign. Later in the same year he found himself fighting at the famous Battle of Omdurman under General Kitchener who routed the Dervish forces of the Sudan who had murdered the heroic General Gordon. The British had set out to punish the rebels for this act, and Winston took part in the last cavalry charge that the British army undertook. The fighting lasted five hours. Only 25 British soldiers were killed and only 136 were wounded. But the Dervish army lost 10,000 men. 16,000 of them were wounded, and 5,000 captured. Winston had his first taste of the horror of war. It contrasted oddly with his ideas about the glory and honour of battle. His description of wounded men tells its own terrible tale: 'from the

direction of the enemy there came a succession of grisly apparitions; horses spouting blood, struggling on three legs, men staggering on foot, men bleeding from terrible wounds, fish-hook spears stuck right through them, arms and faces cut to pieces, bowels protruding, men gasping, crying, collapsing, expiring.' It was no good closing his eyes and thinking about the glories of armed combat — this horror was the reality of war, the

thing for which Winston had been trained. 'What did it look like?' he asked Admiral Beatty who had been watching the fighting from a nearby gunboat on the Nile. 'It looked like plum duff: brown currants scattered about in a great deal of suet,' said the Admiral cheerfully.

In 1899 Winston resigned his commission as an army officer and looked around for further opportunities.

He had a small private income of £500 a year, and he had been well paid as a war correspondent. He had written best-selling books about the military campaigns he had served in, and he was becoming famous. When he returned from serving with his regiment in India in 1899 he fought a very different sort of campaign — he stood for Parliament as a Conservative candidate at a by-election in Oldham. He lost by 1300 votes. Winston didn't like defeat one little bit, but at least he had made his first foray into politics and he would be back to do battle again in the future. He left the political arena to return to military campaigns. War between the Boer Republic and the British had broken out in South Africa and Winston again found himself a war correspondent's job and sailed for the Cape.

On 15 November he was travelling happily on an

armoured train 22 kilometres out on a reconnaissance from Estcourt when it was ambushed by Boers. Three trucks were derailed and Winston immediately leaped into action. From a nearby ridge, scores of Boers poured heavy rifle fire in the direction of Winston and the trapped soldiers. While the British troops diverted attention by firing a six-pounder naval gun at the enemy, Winston nipped out and ran along the line to the head of the train. Though the engine was still on the rails, the tracks were blocked by two armoured trucks and a bogey that had overturned. Shrapnel rained around him and the wounded men sheltering from the exploding shells that were hurled at them by Boer field guns. Winston decided to detach the engine, topple the trucks blocking the line of retreat, and push the remaining three upright trucks towards the engine to be recoupled.

For over an hour, under a blazing sun, under constant bombardment from exploding shells and the ceaseless hammering of bullets, Winston and 20 men succeeded in the desperate plan. The engine began to crawl slowly back along the line, the three remaining trucks crammed with more than 40 soldiers, most of them streaming with blood, and it soon outstripped the infantry holding out three hundred metres away. Winston forced the engine driver to stop, and jumped out to hurry the rest of the troops up to the train. But the Boers had not been idle, and two men in slouch hats intercepted him, firing their rifles while Winston ducked away up nearby banking and under a wire fence to try to reach cover in the rocky gorge of the

Blue Krantz River. No good. A furiously galloping
rider bore down on him and Winston reached down to
grab for the pistol he kept in his belt. It wasn't there! It
had fallen out when he was clearing the track. There

was nothing else for it: 'I held up my hands and surrendered myself a prisoner of war.'

With 51 of his companions, Winston was marched 95 kilometres to a prisoner-of-war camp in Pretoria where he spent three weeks before managing to escape. He had money and some chocolate, but no map or compass. Even in the heart of enemy country, alone and in danger of being shot on sight, he formed a wild plan. 'I would find the Delgoa Bay railway, board a train in motion and hide under the seats. After two hours I perceived the signal lights of a station and hid in the ditch beyond the platform. Suddenly I heard the whistle and the approaching rattle. The great yellow headlights of the engine drew near, the rattle became a roar. The dark mass hung for a second above me, clouds of steam rushed past. I hurled myself on the trucks, grasped some sort of handhold, was swung off my feet. It was a goods train filled with empty coal bags. I burrowed in among them until I was completely buried.' He slept for a while, and woke suddenly. 'I had to leave the train and find some hiding place while it was still dark. I crawled from my cosy place and sprang. My feet struck the ground in two gigantic strides and the next instant I was sprawling in the ditch, shaken but unhurt. I set out for the hills and entered a small grove of trees to wait until dusk.'

Winston was lucky to meet the manager of a nearby coalmine who was friendly to the British. He was hidden at the bottom of the mine until he could be smuggled out, lying low among bales of wool, on a train that crossed into Portuguese territory which bordered on South Africa. Winston's escape was front page news. When he got back to Durban, which was in English hands, he was treated like a hero and carried shoulder high to the Town Hall. 'I was received as if I had won a great victory . . . sheaves of telegrams from all parts of the world poured in upon me, and I started that night for the Army in a blaze of triumph.' Winston continued to send back reports of the war to British newspapers until the British army entered Pretoria when Winston and his cousin, now 8th Duke of Marlborough, galloped into the town ahead of the army where Winston personally tore down the Boer flag over the prison.

His personal courage and success in South Africa did him no harm when he returned to England to stand again at Oldham as a Conservative candidate for Parliament. This time, in 1900, he won by a majority of only 230 votes. But it was enough. He was about to start another successful career, aged only 26 and already one of the most famous men in the country.

Chapter Three

Winston was a romantic. He loved the traditions and the ceremonies of his country. The wars and battles he had fought were, to his mind, only the latest in a long series of triumphs for the British people who had for centuries defended themselves and spread their power throughout the world. On 15 February 1901, King Edward VII opened the first Parliament of the 20th century and Winston took his seat on the backbenches as a new Member of the House of Commons. One newspaper described him leaning back quite at ease on the long bench, a tall, black silk hat tipped low down across his forehead, his body doubled-up, and both hands in his pocket. He looked as though he was eyeing everyone with all the arrogance of a sixth former inspecting the new boys at the beginning of a new term.

In fact, he was probably as excited and anxious to do well as on his first day at Sandhurst. He knew he had to prove himself all over again. 'It was an honour,' he thought, 'to take part in the deliberations of this famous assembly which for centuries had guided England through numberless perils forward on the path of Empire.' He was worried, too, about having to make his first speech in the House of Commons. He had given a great many speeches in public during his election campaign, but this was different. 'Though I had done nothing else for many months but address large audiences, it was with awe as well as eagerness that I braced myself for what I regarded as the supreme ordeal.' He was confident about making a speech to Parliament only if he had worked hard to rehearse in detail exactly what he was going to say. His ability to memorise long pieces of poetry as a schoolboy came in useful. 'For many years,' he once wrote, 'I was unable to say anything that I had not written out and committed to memory. A newspaper editor remembered him practising his speeches by reading them aloud. 'All day he might be heard booming away in his bedroom, rehearsing his facts and flourishes to the accompaniment of resounding knocks on the furniture.' Winston used not only his great voice, but also his hands and his body. His speeches were always dramatic.

But almost immediately there was trouble. As a member of the Conservative Party, Winston disagreed with his colleagues on the meaning of democracy. He believed in free trade, as his father had done, but the Tories were moving towards a policy of trade protection. Winston spoke out fiercely against his Party's views and on 31 May 1904 he dramatically crossed the floor of the House of Commons to sit on the benches on the other side where the Liberal Party were assembled in opposition to the Conservative government. He had, by this action, abandoned his own Party and thrown in his lot with the Liberals. In the 1906 election the Tories were swept away, out of power.

They had won only 157 seats out of a possible 670. Two years later Winston was made President of the Board of Trade and became a Cabinet Minister for the first time.

As a Member of Parliament and a powerful figure in the Liberal government, Winston made many important friends. He was outspoken and outgoing in his behaviour, and he was determined to serve his party, his constituents and his country to the very best of his ability. He was a warm-hearted man, and on a visit to Manchester he was horrified by the slums of that great city. He determined to try to establish minimum standards of life and work for everyone, to help the poor and the miserable, the old and the unhappy. Winston had been miserable, cruelly treated and oppressed at school. He knew what it was like to be unhappy, and he had a natural sympathy for people who were underprivileged. He plunged into social reform with zest, and successfully helped to put several Acts of Parliament on the statute books that would make sweated labour illegal, and provide money for the old, the sick and the poor. Winston Churchill is one of the fathers of the modern welfare state.

In 1908 he was 33 years old, and on 12 September that year he married a young 23-year-old woman called Clementine Hozier. Winston had fallen in love at first sight with the girl he had known for four years. His 'Clemmie' was one of the most beautiful women in London — also intelligent, fascinated by politics, as high-spirited as Winston himself, and interested in social reform. They were made for one another and in Winston's own words, 'lived happily ever afterwards.'

In 1910, Winston was offered the important job of being Home Secretary. Having been himself a prisoner during the Boer War he was aware of the tremendous boredom of prison life. He made a point of trying to improve conditions in British prisons by encouraging prisoners to take part in educational and other social activities among themselves. But he made mistakes, too. The years at the beginning of the 20th century were not easy for governments. Women were demanding the vote, and many people in the country lived lives of great hardship. Trade unions were making their own demands for social reform, and Winston, though prepared to admit that there was much wrong with the conditions of the working class, was impatient with anyone he thought to be 'idlers and wastrels.'

As Home Secretary, he ordered troops to stand by to support police who had been sent to tackle strikers at Tonypandy and Llanelly in Wales. At Llanelly four rioting strikers were killed, and many people held Winston responsible for their deaths. Government was not, after all, quite the same thing as fighting a military battle. He again called out troops to deal with the strange events that happened in Sidney Street in London's East End. An armed gang of men had murdered some policemen during a burglary and then barricaded themselves in the house. Winston was asked to agree to the use of soldiers to get them out. He not only agreed, but went to the scene himself, unable to resist the excitement. Wearing a top hat and a fur-lined coat, he immediately began to direct the siege

personally and next day he was front page news. King George was furiously angry at the conduct of his government Minister nipping about between bullets and directing operations in person. Winston was not much put down. To objectors, he simply said, 'Don't be cross. It was such fun!'

Women, too, felt that Winston was not on their side. He was opposed to votes for women, and, though he later changed his mind about the subject, in 1910 he was blamed for the rough handling police had given to suffragettes during the 'Battle of Downing Street' on November 22. He was becoming very unpopular both with the people and with his own Party. In only a few years he would find himself, like his father before him, a political outcast.

Chapter Four

The first of the great wars of the 20th century was about to burst over Europe. The first hint of catastrophe came in 1911 with the Agadir crisis when the German Emperor sent his gunboat *Panther* to Agadir in French Morocco to protect German interests there. After a quarrel, the gunboat withdrew, but it was obvious that the Germans were intent on extending their power in the world. In October Winston was given the post of First Lord of the Admiralty and control of the Navy. He lost no time in getting to work to learn every detail of his new responsibilities. He equipped his ships with 15 inch guns, converted the fuelling of ships from coal to oil thereby greatly increasing the Navy's mobility and speed, and set up a crash programme of building new ships. By 1914 the British Navy was the strongest in the world, supreme on the seas, and more than a match for the German fleet. It was ready for anything.

He turned his attention to command of the air. He learned to fly the new aircraft that were to become the Royal Naval Air Service. He battled with old Navy experts who were so stuck in the past that they could not believe that aircraft were of much use to anyone. But Winston saw the possibility of launching aircraft from

the decks of his battleships and of fighting an enemy
from the air. British aircraft were the first to carry
machine guns and to launch torpedos from the air. By
the time war was declared on 4 August 1914, when the
signal 'Commence hostilities against Germany' was
flashed to the ships of the British Navy, Winston almost
single-handedly had made sure that he had sole
command of the sea and the air.

War acted on Winston's personality like a dozen pep-
pills. He wrote to his wife, 'I am interested, geared up
and happy. Is it not horrible to be built like that?' He
was older, now. Almost 40 years old, and he no longer
looked at war with the mind of a young, inexperienced
man. In 1909 he had written, 'Much as war attracts and

fascinates my mind with its tremendous situations, I feel more deeply every year . . . what vile and wicked folly and barbarism it all is.' But when it came to the crunch, he was as excited and enthusiastic as he had ever been. The important thing now was to work, fight, put every ounce of energy into winning.

But the main area of action was on land, not on the seas or in the air. Winston was in sole charge of the entire air defence of Britain against raids by the enormous German Zeppelin airships. He set up a Royal Naval Air Service base at Dunkirk on the northern coast of France and here he had an inspiration. He thought of relieving the stalemate of the Army's trench warfare by using armoured cars that could cross the trenches. Winston was on the point of inventing the tank. He ordered 18 'land ships' to be built at a cost of £70,000 and it is from these early prototypes that the modern tank has developed.

But not all was going well for Winston. After a number of British losses, German escapes at sea, and the Navy's failure to bring the German fleet to battle, two British ships and 1500 men went down at the Battle of Coronel on 1 November 1914. Public confidence in the Navy was failing, and Winston was urging the government to mount campaigns in the Near East at Gallipoli and in the Dardanelles. Had his campaigns succeeded, they would have been brilliant victories. But they fizzled out and Winston's career in the Liberal government was finished. The Liberals and the Conservatives formed a coalition government and the Tories, Winston's enemies after he had deserted them at the start of his

Parliamentary career, would not have him in the
government at any price. Winston was shattered and for
a while from the sidelines he watched all his plans crash
and end in tragedy.

He decided to rejoin the army, to resume a military
career. He was made a colonel, given command of a
battalion in the Sixth Royal Scots Fusiliers, and set off to
fight. He enjoyed himself hugely. Once again bullets
were whizzing past his ears, shells exploded while he
bustled about the front line troops, and he felt that he
was in the thick of things, where (as in Cuba so many
years before) 'real things were going on.' But now and
again he would get up and assert himself as a Member of

Parliament by making a speech demanding more push and effort by politicians to win the war.

Winston was still convinced that he could do more for his country at the heart of power and politics than as food for the enemy cannon. In July 1917 he was reinstated in the Cabinet as Minister of Munitions. He threw himself into the job of building more and more of his tanks. They had been wildly successful; and in 1917, 378 fighting tanks and 98 auxiliary tanks made an attack on the Germans at Cambria. Ten kilometres of German trenches were captured and the tanks proved themselves as a decisive factor in winning the war. Winston also worked to increase the strength of the machine gun

corps and the power of the British air forces. On 11 November 1918 the struggle had been won.

In Winston's own words, 'The mighty framework of German Imperial Power, which a few days before had overshadowed the nations, shivered suddenly into a thousand individually disintegrating fragments. All her Allies, whom she had so long sustained, fell down broken and ruined, begging separately for peace. The faithful armies were beaten at the front and demoralised from the rear. The proud, efficient Navy mutinied. Revolution exploded in the most disciplined and docile of States. The Supreme War Lord fled.' Fled, leaving the British supreme in victory and rejoicing. With his wife, Winston got into his car to go to congratulate the Prime Minister. 'No sooner had we entered our car than 20 people mounted upon it, and in the midst of a wildly cheering multitude we were impelled slowly forward through Whitehall.' Did Winston, perhaps, remember the acclaim he had earned in Durban so long ago, when he was carried shoulder high to the Town Hall as a hero?

Chapter Five

For 21 years, from 1918 to 1939, Europe was at peace. 'The war of the giants' was over and Winston had to find another battle, another enemy. He found it in Russia where there was revolution. In 1919 Winston was in charge of the War Office when 23,000 British and other Allied troops were caught up in the civil war being waged between the forces of the Russian government (the 'Whites') and the Bolshevik rebels led by Lenin (the 'Reds'). Winston was no friend to the Bolsheviks and described Lenin as the embodiment of evil. He was appalled by the atrocities committed by the Russian revolutionaries, and urged the British government to armed intervention against Red Russia. He was not allowed to use men, but he managed to pour arms and supplies into Russia until the British and Allied troops were evacuated. In 1920 Winston tried to ship arms to Poland to help that country in its struggle against the Russians, but he was foiled by dockworkers who refused to load the ships.

Winston was opposed by the Labour Party and by trade unionists who had not forgotten the deaths of four strikers at Llanelly. They threatened a general strike if aid was given to Poland against the Bolsheviks and the

government gave in. The 1922 elections put Winston out of power. He lost his Cabinet post and his seat in Parliament and began to write four books on the First World War. With the money he made from writing, he bought Chartwell, a beautiful manor house in Kent which he loved and worked to improve for the rest of his life. For two years it looked as though he was again finished in politics, but in 1924 his old party, the Conservatives, decided to forgive him for having deserted them and he was elected as the Tory member for Epping. He accepted the post of Chancellor of the Exchequer and for five years was in control of the Treasury. He was not a success, and admitted, 'Everybody said I was the worst Chancellor of the Exchequer that ever was. And I'm now inclined to agree with them.' In 1929 the Labour Party defeated the Conservatives in a general election, and Winston again found himself stripped of political power. He began

43

work on a long history of John Churchill, his ancestor, and when not working on this 'Life of Marlborough' he was planning a 'History of the English Speaking Peoples'. Winston loved history and was a brilliant writer. From books and articles he made a great deal of money and a normal working day began at 7 a.m., often not finishing before 2 or 3 o'clock the next morning. Winston always claimed that he could survive on 5 or 6 hours' sleep, and that a nap in the afternoon for an hour was worth several hours sleep at night. His energy and stamina seemed endless.

Winston continued to keep an eye on world events, and he began to notice worrying signs in Germany. He spoke out in the House of Commons against Germany's demands to be allowed to rearm. He was suspicious of the ambitions of Hitler, the German leader. He knew that Germans resented the loss of their territories after defeat in 1918 and in one speech he told Parliament that 'Equal status is not what Germany is seeking. All these bands of sturdy Teutonic youths, marching through the streets of Germany, with the light of desire in their eyes, are not looking for status. They are looking for weapons; and when they have the weapons, they will then ask for the return of their lost territories.' Winston also noticed that the German air force was about to become stronger than Britain's. He stood almost alone in his fears. Nobody listened to him — he might just as well have been talking to thin air. But the great voice would not be stilled. He continued to thunder.

Meanwhile, Hitler was rousing the German people to think of themselves and their country as the greatest in

Europe. He urged them to assert themselves, and in 1936 Hitler invaded the Rhineland. From that moment Winston knew that war was close. In 1938, Hitler reassured the British Prime Minister, Neville Chamberlain, that after taking over Austria and being given part of Czechoslovakia, he had no more territorial demands to make in Europe. Agreement between the British and the Germans at Munich in 1938 was enough for most of the government. Chamberlain, on his return to London, waved the piece of paper on which was written the agreement with Hitler, and declared it to be proof of 'Peace with honour . . . peace in our time.' Winston didn't believe a word of it. He stood up in Parliament and described the meeting at Munich as a total defeat, a shameful act. He was right. In March 1939 German tanks invaded Prague, the capital of Czechoslovakia. In September 1939 the Nazis poured into Poland and on 4 September Winston was back in his old post as First Lord of the Admiralty and a member of the War Cabinet.

Chapter Six

When war was declared against Germany for the second time in his life and his century, Winston felt the hot blood of battle flow through his veins, and a curious calm fell on his mind. The time of uncertainty was over. He had been proved right in his fears for the future, and there was a job to do. There was a world to be won. Again, he thought back over history and seemed to gain strength from centuries of English and British heroism and adventure. 'I felt a serenity of mind . . . The glory of old England filled my being.' He felt as though he was riding high on his star, far removed from the ordinary cares and struggles of life. His imagination sprang alive, and a great confidence filled his soul. He was 65 years old, and at a time of life when other men would have given up and retired. But Winston found within himself all the strength, fire and courage that he had felt in his first battle as a young man.

In 1940, after 40 years in Parliament, Churchill became Prime Minister of Great Britain. He took command. Writing afterwards about this moment, Winston recalled his profound feelings of relief. 'At last I had the authority to give directions over the whole scene. I felt as if I were walking with Destiny, and that all

my past life had been but a preparation for this hour and for this trial.' He gave himself and his country to the struggle, and he took upon himself the authority and the inspiration to 'speak for England'. Speaking for himself and his people, Winston pledged 'to wage war. War without stint: war to the uttermost. To wage war by sea, land and air, with all our might and with all the strength that God can give to us: to wage war against a monstrous tyranny, never surpassed in the dark, lamentable catalogue of human crime.'

His magnificent voice rolled around the roof of the House of Commons, rallying support from every quarter. If the job was to fight to the uttermost limits of strength, what was to be the outcome? Winston was in no doubt. 'I can answer in one word: it is victory, victory at all costs, victory in spite of terror, victory, however long and hard the road may be.' That it would be a road demanding sacrifice he had again no doubt, and he

47

issued a powerful warning of the misery to come: 'I have nothing to offer but blood, toil, tears and sweat.' But there *was* something else he had to offer, and he gave it generously — his own personal example. His courage, his energy, his will to win and his dedication to his country shone like a blazing beacon in the darkness that fell upon Europe and cast a shadow for six long, dangerous years over the British people.

At the very moment that Winston was offering blood, toil, tears and sweat to Britain, the Germans invaded France. It was 13 May 1940. France fell powerless before the advance of the Nazis. The Allied forces were cut off, powerless, in Belgium. Only one harbour on the northern coast of Europe remained open — Dunkirk. There the men of the British Expeditionary Force were trapped with the sea at their backs and the Germans advancing in force before them. Out of disaster, an event of remarkable heroism occurred. From the jaws of utter defeat, 338,226 British, French and Belgian troops were ferried back to England by 860 craft of all sizes, all kinds and sorts, piloted by anyone who could command a boat. The Channel swarmed with a desperate fleet that, incredibly, snatched a vast military force from the very jaws of the enemy. An enemy that was now at the very gates of an island fortress holding out almost single-handedly against total defeat.

The miraculous evacuation from Dunkirk was no victory, but the heroism and drama of the delivery showed that not all was lost, that the reserves of strength, courage, and the will to win were not yet exhausted, that the struggle against oppression might continue even against the most tremendous odds. Winston shook himself free of despair and began to growl like the fierce old bulldog he so much had grown to resemble. From somewhere deep in his great body he found the voice that roared like a pride of lions, that hurled defiance into the very teeth of the enemy, that twisted the hearts of all that listened to him and set their courage once more to the task of victory. Through tears of grief, in a voice racked by tremendous sobs, Churchill spoke from the very depths of his faith that the enemy would not prevail.

'We shall not flag or fail. We shall go on to the end. We shall fight in France, we shall fight in the seas and oceans . . . we shall defend our island whatever the cost may be. We shall fight on the beaches, we shall fight on the landing-grounds, we shall fight in the fields and in the streets, we shall fight in the hills.' At last the trumpet blast sounded its great note. Winston gathered all his strength to cry: 'We shall NEVER surrender!' As though a tide had turned, he rallied all his force to say the almost unthinkable: 'Even if, which I do not for a moment believe, this island or a large part of it were subjugated and starving, then our empire beyond the seas, armed and guarded by the British Fleet, would carry on the struggle . . . until in God's good time, the New World, with all its power and might, steps forth to the rescue and liberation of the Old.'

Winston was firm that he had done nothing more than to 'speak for England', that 'It was the nation and the race dwelling all round the globe that had the lion's heart. I had the luck to be called upon to give the roar.'

Chapter Seven

France had fallen to the German forces, and on 18 June Winston Churchill spoke again to put their perilous position to the people of Britain. 'The Battle of France is over. I expect that the Battle of Britain is about to begin. Upon this battle depends the survival of Christian civilization. The whole fury and might of the enemy must very soon be turned on us. Hitler knows that he will have to break us in this island or lose the war. If we can stand up to him, all Europe will be free . . . But if we fail, then the whole world will sink into the abyss of a new dark age. Let us therefore brace ourselves to our duties and so bear ourselves that, if the British Empire and its Commonwealth last for a thousand years, men will still say: 'This was their finest hour'.'

The danger was very great. Hitler's plan, code-named 'Operation Sealion', was to destroy the Royal Air Force by hurling the might of the German air force, the Luftwaffe against it and once the skies were swept clean of the British, to send out across the Channel a fleet of barges carrying an army of invaders to storm the beaches of England. A desperate effort was mounted to strengthen the R.A.F. On 13 August, codenamed 'Eagle Day' by the Germans, the Nazis launched the Luftwaffe against British Fighter Command. For three days the Luftwaffe threw almost 2,000 sorties against British Spitfires and Hurricanes that resisted every assault. At the beginning of August 1940 there were almost 1500 British and Allied fighter pilots. By the end of September, losses had reduced this figure to only 840. Winston stood for much of the time in the nerve centre operations room of No. 11 Group, Fighter Command where at one point the map table showed every squadron in the Group engaged in heavy fighting. There was nothing in reserve, and fresh waves of attack were already crossing the coast. Miraculously, the German planes were held off and the R.A.F. still managed to hold a balance of power in the air.

'Never,' said Churchill in amazement and pride, 'Never in the field of human conflict was so much owed by so many to so few.' Baffled by the British resistance, the Luftwaffe continued to attack until mid-September when Hitler finally gave up the effort. He adopted a new tactic: constant, pitiless bombing of London. On 7 September 1,000 bombers dropped their rain of fire and death on the capital city. The destruction was terrible, but the spirit of Londoners rode high. Winston recalled the days of the Blitz when he described how 'night after night 10,000 or 20,000 people were made homeless; when hospitals filled with mutilated men and women were themselves struck by bombs; when hundreds of thousands of weary people crowded together in unsafe and insanitary shelters; when drains were smashed and light, power and gas paralysed; and when, nevertheless, the whole fighting, toiling life of

London had to go forward.' As the terrible, fateful year of 1940 ended, Winston simply recorded: 'We were alive.' Britain had come through. It had survived.

On 7 December 1941, the Japanese bombed the American fleet at Pearl Harbor in Hawaii. By attacking

the United States, the Japanese committed their ally, Hitler, to join their war against America. Roosevelt, the President of the United States, had no choice but to join with Britain in the war against Hitler and the Axis powers. Winston knew that now nothing could prevent victory by the Allies against Hitler.

Earlier in the war, Hitler had also attempted to invade Russia, and now he faced the wrath of the Soviet leader Joseph Stalin and the Russians, the weight of President Roosevelt and the United States, and the undefeated spirit of Churchill and the British people. But the war was far from over. Winston's greatest triumph was ahead of him: D-Day and victory.

On 4 June 1944 the Allies took Rome from the Axis powers, and two days later, 'Operation Overlord' began. The plan was nothing less than the invasion of Europe, a vast, secret, and long-planned operation that plunged British and American troops into France on D-Day — 6 June. At the exact moment when the Allied troops were pouring onto the beaches of Normandy, Churchill coolly announced the facts to a House of Commons taken totally by surprise. Winston's only disappointment was that he had not been allowed to go too. But his plan to take part in the D-Day landings was foiled when the King himself, George VI, insisted on joining his Prime Minister in the adventure. Both of them were persuaded that they could not be spared and reluctantly they both agreed to remain in London.

On 8 May 1945, V.E. (Victory in Europe) Day, Winston spoke to the nation. The Germans had given in, their armies shattered, and on 7 May the cease-fire began. 'The German war is at an end,' said Churchill on radio. 'The evil-doers are now prostrate before us. We may allow ourselves a brief period for rejoicing, but Japan remains unsubdued. Advance, Britannia! Long live the cause of freedom! God save the King!' The nation went wild with joy. As Winston drove to the Commons, he was cheered every inch of the way by crowd upon crowd of rejoicing men, women and children. Speaking to them, Winston beamed and waved. 'God bless you all,' he cried. 'This is *your* victory. In all our long history we have not seen a greater day than this!'

Chapter Eight

Winston Churchill was a warrior, at his best in the very thick of a fight. He was never so successful in peacetime. Eleven weeks after V.E. Day, Winston was defeated in a general election. The leader of the Labour Party, Clement Attlee, became Prime Minister. On the morning of 26 July 1945, he woke 'with a sharp stab of almost physical pain.' The results of the election vote were to be announced, and he was afraid that 'all the pressure of great events, on and against which I had mentally so long maintained my 'flying speed' would cease and I should fall.' In a way, it was hard for him to accept that the high excitement of war was over. He felt like a runner coming to a sharp halt after winning the fastest race of his life.

But perhaps the voters who turned Winston out of 10 Downing Street, the home of Prime Ministers, were right. Winston had done the job he was best suited for and he would have been the wrong man for the monotonous grind of peacetime government. But he had been defeated at the moment of his country's victory and he was hurt. King George VI offered him an honour — the Order of the Garter — but he rejected it, saying he had just been given the order of the boot by the people.

He even later refused a Dukedom, and continued to sit in Parliament as an M.P. and leader of the Opposition party. He was still one of the most respected men in the country and his advice was listened to, particularly his views on foreign affairs. He continued to dislike communism and made speech after speech warning that the West should be ready to defend itself against Soviet Russia.

He was an old man, over 70 years old, but he still worked as hard as ever. He took up his hobbies again — painting and building brick walls at Chartwell, his country house. He wrote, and built up his racing stable of prize-winning horses. He won a Nobel Prize for Literature, was showered with honours, and even, three days before his 74th birthday, rode to hounds with his hat jammed down over his head and the usual cigar stuck in his mouth. On October 26 1951 the Labour Party was defeated in a general election and once again Winston rode back to power as leader of the Conservative Party and Prime Minister of Great Britain. In 1953 he agreed to accept an honour from the new, young monarch, Queen Elizabeth II, who had succeeded to the throne in February 1952 on the death of King George VI, her father. He was knighted and presented with the insignia of the Order of the Garter. Rising from his knee, he was now Sir Winston Churchill.

But Sir Winston was 78 years old, still dogged and determined to go on as a politician and a fighter for as long as possible. He continued as Prime Minister for two more years before stepping down and retiring from public service. He kept his seat in the House of

Commons and, sometimes fast asleep, he could be found in the corner of the front bench below the gangway adjacent to, but not among, the ministers of the Crown. In 1963 he was proclaimed the first honorary citizen of the United States by the American President John

Kennedy. The ceremony in the White House rose
garden was timed so that the BBC could bounce film of it
off the relay satellite, and Sir Winston watched it on
television in Britain. It was a suitable honour — after
all, his mother had been American and Winston always

felt a very special love for the United States.

On 27 February 1964, Sir Winston announced that he would not stand again for election to the House of Commons. On 24 January 1965, at the age of 91, he died after a stroke which caused him to lie in a coma for 14 days. The hero had gone at last to rest, and he was given the soldier's funeral he had asked for. After his body had lain in Westminster Hall for three days, on the fourth day it was carried with solemn pride to St Paul's Cathedral. At 9.45 on 30 January, the body of Sir Winston Churchill was laid upon a gun carriage drawn by 100 sailors of the Royal Navy. He was escorted in death by a detachment of the Royal Air Force. Over the coffin a Union Jack had been draped and on it lay the insignia of the Order of the Garter. Guards of Honour from the Navy, Army and Air Force lined the route from Westminster to the Cathedral. The great, booming chimes of Big Ben were silenced, and a hush fell upon the crowds. There was no cheering now, only grief and mourning and a sense of loss.

Churchill's funeral was an overwhelming spectacle. Eight bands led the procession, and two more followed the coffin on its progress through the streets of London. Waiting for the coffin to arrive was a vast congregation which included the Royal family and representatives from all corners of the world. All the glory, honour, tradition and colour of Great Britain was assembled to do homage to a great patriot and hero. But once the pageantry had risen to its glorious height and faded away, when the last notes of the mighty organ of St Paul's Cathedral had rolled back into history, the old

man returned to his own family. He had wished to be buried in the country churchyard at Bladon beside his mother, his father, and his younger brother Jack.

During the funeral, as Churchill's body had been borne along the flow of the slow-running Thames towards its final resting place in the earth of the country he had loved so well, Winston's old friend General Eisenhower spoke up. He said of his great companion in arms: 'In the coming years, many in countless words will strive to interpret the motives, describe the accomplishments, and extol the virtues of Winston Churchill — soldier, statesman, and citizen that two great countries were proud to claim as their own. Among all the things so written or spoken, there will ring out through all the centuries one incontestable refrain. He was a champion of freedom.'

Winston had won. He had won the world for freedom, he had won the hearts and minds of a great nation, he had won the battles, and he had won his place in history, that great flowing tide of human endeavour that he had seen stretch through the centuries before him and which he saw reach far into the future beyond him.

All quotation is taken from the writings of Winston Churchill, particularly his account of childhood and youth in 'My Early Life', first published in 1930 by Thornton, Butterworth Ltd.